Weekly Reader Children's Book Club presents

YOU'RE THE GUEST OF HONOR, CHARLIE BROWN

Books by Charles M. Schulz

YOU'RE THE GUEST OF HONOR, CHARLIE BROWN

A NEW *PEANUTS* ® BOOK
by Charles M. Schulz

HOLT, RINEHART AND WINSTON
New York • Chicago • San Francisco

Published simultaneously in Canada by Holt, Rinehart
and Winston of Canada, Limited.

First published in book form in 1973.

ISBN: 0-03-011026-2

Library of Congress Catalog Card Number: 73-3700

Printed in the United States of America

This book is a presentation of

The Popcorn Bag

Weekly Reader Book Club Senior Division

Weekly Reader Book Division offers book clubs for
children from preschool to young adulthood. All
quality hardcover books are selected by a distinguished
Weekly Reader Selection Board.

For further information write to:
Weekly Reader Book Division
1250 Fairwood Avenue
Columbus, Ohio 43216

Weekly Reader Children's Book Club Edition

Publisher's edition: $2.95

WHAT A STUPID QUESTION!

WHY WOULD I FORGET THE ROOT BEER AND THE OLIVES?

WOW!! I CAN'T BELIEVE IT!

WHAT A NIGHT...

THAT WOODSTOCK GIVES SOME WILD PARTIES!

IT HAS BEEN FORTY-FIVE MINUTES SINCE I FIRST CAME INTO SCHOOL THIS MORNING...

I FIND, UNFORTUNATELY, THAT I AM NOT ANY SMARTER NOW THAN WHEN I ARRIVED....IF IT IS TRUE THAT NATURE ABHORS A VACUUM, I MAY EVEN BE A LITTLE DUMBER!! NOW, THEREFORE, I WOULD LIKE TO...

YES, MA'AM?

RATS! I HAD A PRETTY GOOD SPEECH GOING THERE FOR A MINUTE!

THE OLDEN DAYS WERE BETTER..

IN THE OLDEN DAYS, MEN USED TO WALK BY WITH TALL BLACK HATS ON, AND KIDS USED TO THROW SNOWBALLS AT THEM

BAD SHOW, LADS!

SCHULZ

Dear Joe Shlabotnik,
How would you like
to be our Master
of Ceremonies?

We are having a
testimonial dinner for our
manager who is also your
number-one fan.

WON'T IT BE GREAT IF HE CAN COME? JOE SHLABOTNIK IS CHARLIE BROWN'S FAVORITE BASEBALL PLAYER...

HE PROBABLY WON'T BE ABLE TO GET AWAY...THEY'RE PRETTY BUSY DOWN AT THE CAR WASH!

IT'S GOING TO BE A TESTIMONIAL DINNER FOR CHARLIE BROWN

I KNOW HIM... THE ROUND-HEADED KID..

IT'S TO SHOW OUR APPRECIATION FOR ALL HE'S DONE AS OUR TEAM MANAGER

I HATE SHOWING APPRECIATION

ANYWAY, YOU'RE INVITED SO PLEASE TRY TO COME..

I WON'T GO UNLESS I CAN SIT AT THE HEAD TABLE!

LOOK! I RECEIVED AN ANSWER FROM JOE SHLABOTNIK!

"DEAR FRIENDS, I ACCEPT YOUR INVITATION TO ATTEND THE TESTIMONIAL DINNER FOR MR. BROWN.. MY USUAL FEE FOR SUCH AFFAIRS IS ONE HUNDRED DOLLARS"

ONE HUNDRED DOLLARS?!! TELL HIM THAT ALL WE CAN AFFORD IS FIFTY CENTS..

"P.S. I'LL TAKE IT!"

HOW ARE PLANS GOING FOR THE BIG TESTIMONIAL DINNER, LINUS?

GREAT! HAVE YOU EVER HEARD OF JOE SHLABOTNIK? HE WAS LAST-ROUND DRAFT CHOICE IN THE GREEN GRASS LEAGUE...

HE'S GOING TO BE OUR GUEST SPEAKER

HOW APPROPRIATE!

ALL RIGHT, GIRLS, LET'S SETTLE DOWN!

THE MEETING WILL COME TO ORDER!

AS MEMBERS OF THE FOOD COMMITTEE, WE HAVE TO DECIDE WHAT TO SERVE AT CHARLIE BROWN'S TESTIMONIAL DINNER...

IS THERE SUCH A THING AS A LOSER'S SALAD?

OKAY, MARCIE, YOU AND I ARE THE INVITATION COMMITTEE

NOW, HERE'S A LIST OF ALL THE PEOPLE WHO ARE TO RECEIVE INVITATIONS TO CHARLIE BROWN'S TESTIMONIAL DINNER.... AT THE BOTTOM OF EACH ONE, WE PUT R.S.V.P.

WHAT DOES R.S.V.P. MEAN, SIR?

"REVISED STANDARD VERSION, PLEASE"

I NEVER UNDERSTAND YOUR JOKES, SIR...

STOP CALLING ME "SIR"!

WE'VE ADDRESSED A LOT OF INVITATIONS, HAVEN'T WE, SIR?

I THINK I'M GETTING SICK FROM LICKING ALL THESE STAMPS AND ENVELOPES

BY GOLLY, THAT STUPID CHUCK BETTER APPRECIATE ALL THE WORK WE'RE DOING TO GIVE HIM THIS TESTIMONIAL DINNER..BESIDES, HE'S A TERRIBLE BALL PLAYER...

IF WE DON'T BELIEVE IN WHAT WE'RE DOING, AREN'T WE BEING HYPOCRITICAL, SIR?

I HATE QUESTIONS LIKE THAT!

THERE'S STILL QUITE A BIT OF WORK TO DO ON THE TESTIMONIAL DINNER...

I WAS WONDERING IF YOU'D CARE TO SERVE ON THE FLOWER COMMITTEE...

SO MUCH FOR THE FLOWER COMMITTEE!

HELLO, CHUCK? AS CHAIRWOMAN OF THE INVITATION COMMITTEE, I HAVE A SURPRISE FOR YOU!

I COULDN'T TELL YOU BEFORE BECAUSE THIS HAS ALL BEEN VERY HUSH-HUSH, BUT NOW I CAN TELL YOU...GUESS WHAT...WE'RE GOING TO GIVE YOU A TESTIMONIAL DINNER!!

HOW DOES THAT HIT YOU CHUCK? ARE YOU EXCITED? ARE YOU SMILING, CHUCK?

I'M SMILING!!!

WHAT'S THE MATTER WITH YOU, BIG BROTHER?

YOU LOOK LIKE YOU JUST SWALLOWED A CHOCOLATE CAKE...

THEY'RE GOING TO GIVE ME A TESTIMONIAL DINNER!

ALL THE KIDS THAT I PLAY BASEBALL WITH ARE GOING TO GIVE ME A TESTIMONIAL DINNER!

CHECK THE CALENDAR...IT MUST BE APRIL FOOL'S DAY!

WELCO CANCEL THE DINNER?

WE CAN'T CANCEL THE DINNER!! EVERYONE IS ALREADY HERE! EVERYONE IS ALREADY SEATED! EVEN THE GUEST OF HONOR IS HERE!!

IT'S ALL HYPOCRITICAL...WE'RE NOT REALLY SINCERE...WE'RE ALL GOING TO SAY THINGS ABOUT CHARLIE BROWN THAT WE DON'T REALLY BELIEVE, AND IT'S ALL HYPOCRITICAL!

I WOULD HAVE ENJOYED EVEN A HYPOCRITICAL DINNER

WHO IN THE WORLD COULD BE CALLING AT THREE O'CLOCK IN THE MORNING?

WHO? NO, THE DINNER WAS CANCELED...WELL, IT'S A LONG STORY...

YES, WE WERE WONDERING WHAT HAD HAPPENED TO YOU...I'M SORRY YOU GOT LOST...ALL RIGHT...MAYBE NEXT TIME...

GOOD NIGHT, MR. SHLABOTNIK

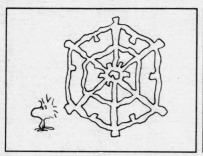

SURPRISE!

WHAT'S THIS?

FRENCH TOAST! I MADE IT MYSELF

BLEAH!! IT TASTES AWFUL!

REALLY?

MAYBE I SHOULDN'T HAVE MADE IT WITH CHOCOLATE MILK...

SCHULZ

"A PINCH-HITTER MAY BE DESIGNATED TO BAT FOR THE STARTING PITCHER AND ALL SUBSEQUENT PITCHERS IN ANY GAME WITHOUT OTHERWISE AFFECTING THE STATUS OF THE PITCHERS IN THE GAME.."

"FAILURE TO DESIGNATE A PINCH-HITTER PRIOR TO THE GAME PRECLUDES THE USE OF A DESIGNATED PINCH-HITTER FOR THE GAME... PINCH-HITTERS FOR A DESIGNATED PINCH-HITTER MAY BE USED..."

"ANY SUBSTITUTE PINCH-HITTER FOR A DESIGNATED PINCH-HITTER HIMSELF BECOMES A DESIGNATED PINCH-HITTER... A REPLACED DESIGNATED PINCH-HITTER SHALL NOT RE-ENTER THE GAME"

I PROBABLY WON'T GET TO BAT THE WHOLE SEASON...

SCHULZ

I FIND IT DIFFICULT TO BELIEVE THAT HE WAS CALLED TO THE WHITE COURTESY TELEPHONE!

FORGET IT!

"TO BE ELIGIBLE FOR THE DAISY HILL PUPPY CUP, NOMINEE MUST FILL OUT THE ENCLOSED FORM"

Name of Owner _____

?

CHARLIE BROWN!!!

HOW EMBARRASSING..

SO THE DAISY HILL PUPPY CUP IS AWARDED TO THE OUTSTANDING NEIGHBORHOOD DOG OF THE YEAR..

YOU'RE GOING TO HAVE SOME PRETTY STRONG COMPETITION

WHAT MAKES YOU THINK YOU CAN WIN?

I'M SO CUTE!

HERE ARE SOME MORE RULES ABOUT THE DAISY HILL PUPPY CUP AWARD

"EACH NOMINEE MUST SUBMIT FIVE LETTERS FROM INTERESTED PARTIES STATING WHY HE SHOULD BE NAMED 'THE NEIGHBORHOOD DOG OF THE YEAR'"

DON'T ASK **ME** TO WRITE A LETTER FOR YOU! I WOULDN'T RECOMMEND YOU FOR "DOG OF THE MINUTE"!

WHAAH!

AND CRYING WON'T HELP!!

I would like to recommend my dog for the Daisy Hill Puppy Cup.

He is brave and loyal and

SNAP SNAP

impatient

YOU KNOW WHAT MAKES KIND OF A GOOD HOBBY? SAVING STRING!

CRUNCH

I DID IT!

I'M IN THE ALPHA STATE!

MOST BIRDS LAND BETWEEN THE LITTLE POINTY THINGS...

YOU JUST THINK YOU'RE CUTE BECAUSE YOU'RE CUTE!

YOU KNOW WHAT?

WHEN I'M WITH YOU, I'M SO HAPPY THAT I'M AFRAID MY HEART IS GOING TO POP

DON'T WORRY ABOUT IT..

NO ONE HAS EVER DIED OF "HEART POP"!

OH,
NO!

I KNEW THIS WAS GOING
TO HAPPEN SOMETIME...

MY BLANKET HAS
BEEN RECALLED!

He was a very
rich cowboy.

He had a car
and a horse.

He kept his car in
the carport....

And he kept his horse
in the horseport.

A NEW MONTH AGAIN..

TODAY IS APRIL FOOL'S DAY, CHARLIE BROWN..

I THINK I'LL PLAY A LITTLE JOKE ON YOU...I THINK I'LL TRY A LITTLE TRICK...

YOU UNDERSTAND WHAT I'M SAYING, DON'T YOU? YOU UNDERSTAND THAT THIS IS APRIL FOOL'S DAY? YOU'RE SURE? I WANT TO BE CERTAIN THAT YOU UNDERSTAND! OKAY?

HEY, CHARLIE BROWN, GUESS WHAT! THAT LITTLE RED-HAIRED GIRL IS OUTSIDE, AND SHE WANTS TO GIVE YOU A HUG AND A KISS!!

REALLY?

WOW! THIS IS FANTASTIC!

APRIL FOOL!

JUST LIKE SHOOTING FISH IN A BARREL!

POWER TO MY KIND!

THIS IS THE MOMENT I WAIT FOR ALL WINTER LONG...

IT'S A STRANGE FEELING WHEN YOU WALK UP ONTO THE MOUND FOR THE FIRST TIME EACH SPRING..

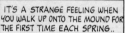

SORT OF GIVES YOU A FEELING OF POWER, EH, CHARLIE BROWN?

OH, NO, IT'S MORE A FEELING OF.... WELL, IT'S KIND OF HARD TO DESCRIBE..

I'D THINK IT WOULD BE A FEELING OF POWER..

NO, I THINK IT'S MORE A FEELING OF NEWNESS...AFTER ALL, IT'S A NEW SEASON AND A NEW BALL GAME...IT'S THAT KIND OF FEELING..

NOT POWER?

IT'S ALSO A FEELING OF BEING PART OF A GREAT TRADITION

I SHOULD THINK THERE'D BE SORT OF A FEELING OF POWER

I THINK IT'S SOMETHING THAT HAS TO BE EXPERIENCED

LET ME TRY...WILL YOU LET ME TRY?

OH, YES, CHARLIE BROWN... I SEE WHAT YOU MEAN!

IT GIVES YOU A FEELING OF POWER!

＊SIGH＊

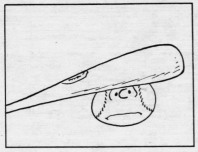

"YES, SIR, I'M THE TEAM MANAGER AND THIS IS OUR SECOND BASEMAN, LINUS VAN PELT..

AND YOU'RE THE LEAGUE PRESIDENT? WE'RE VERY GLAD TO KNOW YOU, SIR

YOU HAVE A VERY NICE BICYCLE REPAIR SHOP HERE

ONE OF MY GREAT REGRETS IS THAT I NEVER GOT TO MEET JUDGE KENESAW MOUNTAIN LANDIS!

SOMETHING WAS WRONG WITH OUR FIRST GAME?

BUT WE WON IT, SIR! WE WON IT FAIR AND SQUARE! THAT'S THE FIRST GAME WE'VE EVER WON!

YOU SAY A GROUP OF PARENTS GOT TOGETHER? BUT WHY?!

IN ALL THIS WORLD, CHARLIE BROWN, THERE IS NOTHING MORE FRIGHTENING THAN THE GETTING TOGETHER OF A GROUP OF PARENTS!

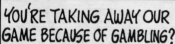

RERUN, YOU REALLY LET ME DOWN!

I WAS THE ONE WHO TALKED CHARLIE BROWN INTO LETTING YOU PLAY; SO THEN YOU GO AND GET US INVOLVED IN A BETTING SCANDAL!

I ONLY BET A NICKEL...WHAT ELSE CAN YOU DO WITH A NICKEL THESE DAYS?

OF COURSE, I MUST ADMIT ONE THING...

YOU'RE THE FIRST PERSON WHO EVER HAD THE COURAGE TO BET ON CHARLIE BROWN'S TEAM

I'LL DRINK TO THAT!

THERE'S ONE THING I STILL DON'T UNDERSTAND..

RERUN BET A NICKEL THAT OUR TEAM WOULD WIN...

WHO DID HE BET WITH?

WHO BET AGAINST US?

HE'S COMING! HE'S COMING!

THANK YOU, EASTER BEAGLE! THANK YOU!

THANK YOU

THANK YOU VERY MUCH

THANK YOU

THANK YOU!

EVERYBODY GETS AN EGG FROM THE EASTER BEAGLE

WHO DO I GET ONE FROM?

HIS ASSISTANT!

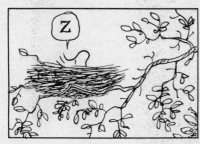

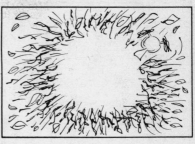

The Bunnies - A Tale of Mirth and Woe.

"Ha Ha Ha," laughed the bunnies.

"Ha Ha Ha Ha Ha Ha Ha Ha Ha Ha Ha Ha"

SO MUCH FOR THE MIRTH!

SLEEPING AGAIN

I DON'T SEE WHY YOU NEED SO MUCH REST

I NEED PLENTY OF REST IN CASE TOMORROW IS A GREAT DAY..

IT PROBABLY WON'T BE, BUT IF IT IS, I'LL BE READY!

WOODSTOCK IS REALLY INTO HOPSCOTCH

CLICK!
PLUNK!

HEE
HEE
HEE
HEE
HEE

STUPID BIRD!

WHAT'S SO GREAT ABOUT WINNING THIRTY GAMES OF EIGHT-BALL IN A ROW?

HEE
HEE
HEE
HEE

I'M SORT OF CURIOUS ABOUT SOMETHING..

DO YOU THINK YOU'LL EVER GET MARRIED, CHUCK?

OH, I SUPPOSE SO...JUST ABOUT EVERYONE DOES...

WHAT KIND OF GIRL DO YOU THINK YOU'LL MARRY?

WELL, I ALWAYS KIND OF HATE TO TALK ABOUT THOSE THINGS BECAUSE IT MAY SOUND SILLY, BUT I'D LIKE A GIRL WHO WOULD CALL ME, "POOR, SWEET BABY"

POOR, SWEET BABY?!!

UH, HUH!

IF I WAS FEELING TIRED, OR DEPRESSED OR SOMETHING LIKE THAT, SHE'D CUDDLE UP CLOSE TO ME, KISS ME ON THE EAR AND WHISPER, "POOR, SWEET BABY"

FORGET IT, CHUCK... IT'LL NEVER HAPPEN!

SMAK!

POOR, SWEET BABY!

DO YOU REALIZE THAT YOU'VE WALKED THIRTY-FIVE BATTERS IN A ROW?

I'M SORRY... I JUST CAN'T HELP IT... I CAN'T GET THE BALL OVER THE PLATE...

I'M NOT COMPLAINING...

ACTUALLY, I'M GETTING A LOT OF LETTERS WRITTEN!

YOU DON'T THINK I CARE ABOUT ALL THE GAMES WE LOSE, DO YOU, CHARLIE BROWN?

WELL, I'LL HAVE YOU KNOW THAT I SPEND A LOT OF TIME OUT HERE IN CENTER FIELD, AND MOST OF IT IS SPENT CRYING...

SEE? THE GRASS IS EXTRA GREEN ALL AROUND THIS SPOT WHERE I STAND AND WATER IT WITH MY TEARS...

THAT'S VERY TOUCHING..

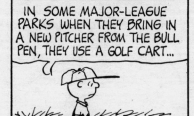

OLGA KORBUT HAS BEEN BUGGING ME FOR LESSONS!

DO YOU LIKE ME MORE THAN I LIKE YOU, CHUCK?

I DON'T KNOW...DO YOU LIKE ME MORE THAN I LIKE YOU?

LET'S NOT PLAY LOVERS' GAMES, CHUCK!

Dear Contributor,
We regret to inform you that your manuscript does not suit our present needs.   The Editors

STOMP! STOMP!
STOMP! STOMP!

P.S. Don't take it out on your mailbox.

MOM?

SNIF!

THAT'S THE SADDEST THING I'VE EVER SEEN.. ESPECIALLY ON MOTHER'S DAY...

OF COURSE, WHO AM I TO TALK?

I DON'T KNOW WHERE MY MOM IS EITHER... I DON'T KNOW WHERE MY DAD IS OR ANY OF MY BROTHERS OR SISTERS..

THAT'S TERRIBLE..

WHERE IS EVERYBODY?

SCHULZ

I FIND IT DIFFICULT TO BELIEVE THAT GOD REALLY CARES WHO WINS A GOLF TOURNAMENT!

MY DAD IS PLAYING IN A CANCER FUND GOLF TOURNAMENT TOMORROW...

MY MOM IS PLAYING IN A TENNIS TOURNAMENT NEXT WEEK FOR THE KIDNEY FOUNDATION...

WE SHOULD HOLD A BENEFIT BASEBALL TOURNAMENT

THAT'S A GREAT IDEA!

I CAN SEE IT NOW... "CHARLIE BROWN'S FLU TOURNAMENT!"

HELLO, PEPPERMINT PATTY?

HI, CHUCK! GEE, WHAT A SURPRISE... HOW'VE Y'BEEN?

FINE, THANK YOU... I'LL GET RIGHT TO THE POINT...HOW ABOUT YOUR TEAM PLAYING OUR TEAM IN A BENEFIT BASEBALL GAME, YOU KNOW, LIKE THEY HAVE FOR HEART ASSOCIATIONS AND THINGS?

WHAT WOULD OUR GAME BE FOR, CHUCK, THE COMMON COLD?

IF WE'RE GOING TO HAVE A CHARITY BASEBALL GAME, CHARLIE BROWN, IT SHOULD BE FOR A WORTHY CAUSE..

HOW ABOUT HEADACHES? NO ONE EVER HAS A BENEFIT FOR HEADACHES...

HOW ABOUT SORE THROATS? OR HOW ABOUT CUT FINGERS AND SKINNED KNEES?

IF OUR TEAM IS GOING TO BE PLAYING, IT SHOULD BE FOR STOMACH-ACHES!

I CAN'T STAND IT!

GUESS WHAT, MARCIE...OUR TEAM IS GOING TO PLAY CHUCK'S TEAM IN A CHARITY BASEBALL GAME!

BUT I'M NOT ON YOUR TEAM, SIR... I DON'T PLAY BASEBALL...

WE DON'T WANT YOU TO PLAY MARCIE..WE WANT YOU TO SELL TICKETS!

YOU MEAN GO FROM DOOR TO DOOR?

SURE

WHAT IF I GET MUGGED?

OKAY, MARCIE, HERE ARE THE TICKETS...GET OUT THERE, AND SELL THEM!

THESE TICKETS COST FIFTY CENTS, SIR...WHO'S GOING TO PAY FIFTY CENTS TO WATCH CHUCK'S TEAM PLAY BALL?

YOURS IS NOT TO REASON WHY, MARCIE! YOURS IS TO SELL TICKETS! THIS IS FOR CHARITY!

I'M SORRY, SIR... I GUESS I'M ALWAYS "REASONING WHY"

STOP CALLING ME "SIR"!

I'M A FAILURE, SNOOPY...I DIDN'T SELL A SINGLE TICKET!

POOR, SWEET BABY!

SMAK!

WELL, THERE GOES OUR CHARITY BASEBALL GAME! IF NO ONE BUYS A TICKET, WE MIGHT AS WELL CALL IT OFF...

RATS! I NEVER DO ANYTHING RIGHT... NOTHING EVER WORKS OUT FOR ME...

POOR, SWEET BABY!

SMAK!

HE ADMITTED IT, AND I FORGAVE HIM...

BUT I STILL DON'T THINK A FRIEND SHOULD EAT THE HEAD OFF YOUR CHOCOLATE BUNNY!

"Hi, pretty girl," he said.

"I love you," she said, and together they laughed. Then one day she said, "I hate you," and they cried. But not together.

"What happened to the love that we said would never die?" she asked. "It died," he said.

The first time he saw her she was playing tennis. The last time he saw her she was playing tennis.

"Ours was a Love set," he said, "but we double-faulted." "You always talked a better game than you played," she said.

THAT'S VERY GOOD...NOW ALL YOU NEED IS A TITLE...

A Love Story by Erich Beagle

Dear Contributor,
We are returning
your stupid story.

You are a terrible writer.
Why do you bother us?
We wouldn't buy one of your
stories if you paid us.

Leave us alone. Drop
dead. Get lost.

PROBABLY A FORM
REJECTION SLIP...

flitter
flitter
flutter
flitter

flitter
flitter
SPUT
SPUT
flutter
flutter
SPUT
SPUT
SPUT

BOING!!

EJECTED
JUST IN
TIME!

I WONDER WHERE MY FATHER IS...

THAT'S THE TROUBLE WITH BEING A DOG...THEY TAKE YOU AWAY FROM YOUR FAMILY, AND SELL YOU TO SOME STUPID KID AND YOU NEVER SEE YOUR MOM AND DAD AGAIN!

"BUT YOU GET TO LIVE WITH A HUMAN FAMILY," THEY SAY... HA! BIG DEAL! SOME CHOICE!

YOU DON'T EVEN **GET** A CHOICE! YOU GO WHERE THEY SEND YOU! HUMANS DRIVE ME CRAZY! JUST THINKING ABOUT IT MAKES ME SO MAD I COULD...

SUPPERTIME!

CHOMP GULP! CHOMP GULP! CHOMP GULP!

BONK!

NOW, WHAT BROUGHT **THAT** ON?

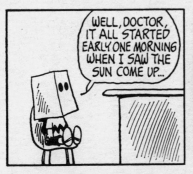

WHAT ARE YOU PACKING FOR, BIG BROTHER?

MY DOCTOR SAYS I SHOULD GO TO CAMP...HE SAID I HAVE TO DO SOMETHING THAT WILL TAKE MY MIND OFF BASEBALL

I'VE SEEN YOU PLAY.. I NEVER THOUGHT YOU HAD YOUR MIND ON IT!

THANKS A LOT... I'LL SEE YOU IN TWO WEEKS...

YOU'RE GOING TO BE A BIG HIT AT CAMP CARRYING YOUR HEAD IN A SACK!!

SCHULZ

SO HERE I AM ON A BUS GOING TO CAMP...

FOR SOMEONE WHO HATES GOING TO CAMP, I SURE SPEND A LOT OF TIME THERE... MAYBE I WENT TO THE WRONG DOCTOR...

EVERY SUMMER HE DRAGS HIS FAMILY OFF ON A FIVE-WEEK CAMPING TRIP...HIS SOLUTION FOR EVERYTHING IS "GO TO CAMP!"

I KNOW WHAT'LL HAPPEN TO ME.. JUST WHEN I GET OLD ENOUGH WHERE I WON'T HAVE TO GO ANY MORE, I'LL GET DRAFTED INTO THE INFANTRY!

SCHULZ

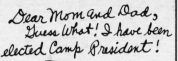

Dear Mom and Dad,
Guess What! I have been
elected Camp President!

MR. SACK, EXCUSE ME, BUT DO YOU THINK I SHOULD SIGN UP FOR NATURE HIKE OR FOR SWIMMING?

SWIMMING, DEFINITELY!! NATURE HIKES ARE GREAT, BUT LEARNING TO SWIM IS A MUST!

THANK YOU, MR. SACK... YOU SURE ARE SMART!

Life here in camp
is wonderful.

YEARS AGO THERE WAS A CARTOON DRAWN BY FRANK WING ABOUT FISHING...

THIS BOY WAS HELPING HIS DAD HOE THE GARDEN, AND HE SAID, "GEE, PA, I'LL BET THE FISH ARE BITIN' GOOD TODAY," AND HIS DAD SAID, "UH HUH, AN' IF YOU STAY WHERE YOU'RE AT, THEY WON'T BITE YOU!"

THAT'S VERY FUNNY, MR. SACK

I ALWAYS LIKED THAT CARTOON

YOU'RE FUN TO BE WITH, MR. SACK

THANK YOU

MY HEAD DOESN'T SEEM TO ITCH ANY MORE...MAYBE MY RASH HAS GONE AWAY...

IF IT HAS, I COULD TAKE THIS STUPID GROCERY SACK OFF MY HEAD...OF COURSE, THEN I PROBABLY WOULDN'T BE CAMP PRESIDENT ANY MORE, EITHER...

ON THE OTHER HAND, I CAN'T WEAR THIS SACK FOR THE REST OF MY LIFE...

IF I EVER WENT TO A GROCERY STORE, AND THE CLERK YELLED, "CARRY OUT!" I'D END UP IN THE BACK OF SOME STATION WAGON!

PSST, MR. SACK... WHAT ARE YOU DOING UP SO EARLY?

I'M GOING OUT TO WATCH THE SUN RISE...IF IT'S THE SUN, I'LL KNOW I'M CURED...IF IT'S A BASEBALL, I'M STILL IN TROUBLE..

?? HE DIDN'T HAVE A SACK OVER HIS HEAD ??!??

HE IS OUR CAMP PRESIDENT ?!?

ANOTHER GAME TODAY...IF WE WIN, WE'LL ONLY BE TEN GAMES OUT OF SEVENTH PLACE...

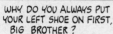

WHY DO YOU ALWAYS PUT YOUR LEFT SHOE ON FIRST, BIG BROTHER?

WELL, ACTUALLY, I DON'T...I ONLY PUT IT ON FIRST ON DAYS WHEN WE HAVE A BASEBALL GAME...

I GUESS IT'S KIND OF A SUPERSTITION... BASEBALL PLAYERS HAVE A LOT OF SUPERSTITIONS..

WHAT WOULD HAPPEN IF YOU DIDN'T DO IT?

WELL, WE'D PROBABLY LOSE THE GAME

HAVE YOU EVER WON?

WHERE'S OUR PITCHER?

I DON'T KNOW...I HAVEN'T SEEN HIM..

!?

I DON'T UNDERSTAND...THE GAME IS READY TO START, AND YOU'RE STILL SITTING HERE IN YOUR BEDROOM WITHOUT YOUR SHOES ON!

I'VE NEVER SEEN IT TO FAIL!

FIND A GOOD SPOT, AND EVERYONE ELSE MOVES IN!

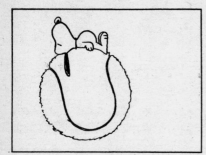

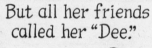

THAT JUST DOESN'T WORK..

I HAVE TO SLEEP IN THE SAME DIRECTION THAT THE WORLD TURNS

I HATE SLEEPING IN WOODSTOCK'S GUEST ROOM!

ALL RIGHT, GOLF FANS, THIS IS IT... THE OLD PRO HAS TO MAKE THIS ONE...

HE'S DOWN TO THE LAST PUTT, AND HE CAN'T PLAY IT SAFE... HE HAS TO GO FOR IT...

THERE'S NO TOMORROW!

THERE'S NO TOMORROW?!

THERE'S NO TOMORROW!!

THEY JUST ANNOUNCED ON TV THAT THERE'S **NO TOMORROW!!!**

THERE'S NO TOMORROW!! THEY JUST ANNOUNCED IT ON TV!

PANIC! PANIC! RUN! HIDE! FLEE! RUN FOR THE HILLS! FLEE TO THE VALLEYS! RUN TO THE ROOF TOPS!

SOMEHOW I NEVER THOUGHT IT WOULD END THIS WAY!

I THOUGHT ELIJAH WAS TO COME FIRST...

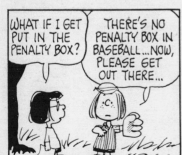

I HAVE THE BALL, SIR... WHAT DO YOU WANT ME TO DO WITH IT?

OKAY, MARCIE, IT'S YOUR TURN AT THE PLATE..

I DON'T UNDERSTAND BASEBALL EXPRESSIONS, SIR...

STOP CALLING ME 'SIR', AND BELT ONE!

HERE, YOU'LL DO BETTER USING A BAT...

WHY DO THEY MAKE THE HANDLES SO BIG, SIR?

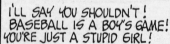

Though her husband often went on business trips, she hated to be left alone.

"I've solved our problem," he said. "I've bought you a St. Bernard. It's name is Great Reluctance."

"Now, when I go away, you shall know that I am leaving you with Great Reluctance!"

She hit him with a waffle iron.

OVERHEAD SMASH!

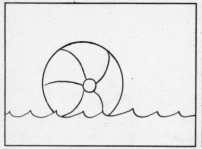

THE WORST THING ABOUT SWIMMING IS CROSSING A HOT PARKING LOT!

BASIC
KARATE
HANDBOOK

BASIC
KARATE
HANDBOOK

Fred Neff

Photographs by James E. Reid

Lerner Publications Company
Minneapolis

The models photographed in this book are Mike Podolinsky, Bruce Bottomley, Bill Polta, Laura Phillips, Rick Rowell, and Jack Engelhart.

LIBRARY OF CONGRESS CATALOGING IN PUBLICATION DATA

Neff, Fred.
  Basic karate handbook.

  (Fred Neff's Self-Defense Library)
  Includes index.
  SUMMARY: Introduces basic karate techniques and includes a history, warm-up exercises, and answers to common questions on self-defense.

  1. Karate—Juvenile literature. [1. Karate] I. Title.

GV1114.3.N44 1976   796.8'153   75-38471
ISBN 0-8225-1150-9

Manufactured in the United States of America

International Standard Book Number: 0-8225-1150-9
Library of Congress Catalog Card Number: 75-38471

9   10   94   93   92   91

CONTENTS

This book is dedicated to all my students.

PREFACE

When I became a student of karate in the 1950s, few Americans had knowledge of the Oriental fighting arts or were interested in learning them. Since that time, however, public interest in the subject has grown considerably. Today, thousands of people all over the country are studying the various fighting arts and are learning that they offer many physical, psychological, and social benefits.

This new interest and involvement in the Oriental fighting arts has created a need for books that can be used as instructional guides for beginning students. FRED NEFF'S SELF-DEFENSE LIBRARY was written to help meet that need. My purpose in writing the series was to provide a basic comprehensive course on self-defense, based on the major Oriental disciplines of karate, judo, and jujitsu. In preparing each book, I was careful to include not only the physical techniques of Oriental fighting but also the underlying philosophical principles. This is important because an understanding of both elements is required of every martial arts student. Finally, in selecting the particular self-defense techniques for each book, I tried to include techniques that could be of practical use to the average person and that could be performed effectively and safely through practice. I genuinely hope that each and every reader of the SELF-DEFENSE LIBRARY benefits as much as I have from studying the martial arts.

Fred Neff

INTRODUCTION

Karate is an ancient Oriental fighting art that teaches self-defense and physical conditioning. Its major goal is to teach students how to effectively use their bodies as weapons in self-defense situations. (The Japanese word *karate* actually means "empty hand" in English.) In karate, the hands, elbows, knees, and feet are all used for self-defense fighting. Students use these body areas according to the basic fighting techniques that karate teaches. These techniques include dodges and blocks, punches and strikes, and kicks. All of the self-defense techniques are based on sound principles of body mechanics. Through faithful practice of the techniques, students can greatly increase their strength and effectiveness for self-defense.

The art of karate also teaches a philosophy of self-defense. It is important that students understand this philosophy and live by it if they are to use their knowledge of karate effectively. The philosophy is based on the practice of self-control. Karate students should never allow verbal threats or challenges to draw them into a fight. Only if they are in real physical danger should students use their self-defense training, and then only to stop the fight right away. Because a knowledge of karate gives a person a physical advantage over others, that knowledge must be handled wisely. Karate teaches that along with increased strength and skill goes a greater responsibility to show kindness toward others and to avoid trouble.

HISTORY OF KARATE

The Oriental fighting arts have been in existence for over three thousand years. The Chinese are often credited with being the first to practice the art of karate. It was the religious leaders, or monks, of ancient China who first developed the techniques of empty-hand fighting. They used these techniques to protect themselves from the brutal attackers they sometimes met while traveling the country to spread their religious teachings. As they developed and practiced the art, the monks discovered that karate was excellent not only for self-defense but also for establishing harmony between mind and body.

At first, the monks practiced karate only in their religious temples. One of the most famous of these temples was the Shaolin temple. The Shaolin monks of the sixth century A.D. were taught a very complete and effective form of self-defense. They were expected to develop themselves physically, mentally, and spiritually. Special emphasis was put on developing self-control, personal sincerity, and kindness toward others.

After a period of years, the monks began to practice karate outside their temples and to teach it to ordinary citizens. This led to the development of many different styles of self-defense, since the individual monks and karate masters differed in their teachings.

Eventually, karate spread from its Chinese homeland to other Asian countries, including Okinawa, Korea, and Japan. In those countries, additional styles of self-defense were developed. Today, the art of karate is practiced worldwide, and thousands of people continue to benefit from its teachings.

COMMON QUESTIONS ON SELF-DEFENSE

It is very important for students to understand the basic philosophy of karate. In order to simplify the presentation of that philosophy, this chapter has been made up of questions and answers. The questions are those frequently asked by beginning karate students. They are therefore of a practical nature, concerning the use of karate in real-life situations. The answers have been designed to give the basic philosophy of karate self-defense. Only through understanding this philosophy and living it will the student of karate be able to use his or her knowledge effectively.

1. When should I use my karate training?

The first rule of karate is that you should use your training only when you are in danger of being physically harmed. Unless this danger exists, there is no need for you to *prove* your strength and skill. Because your knowledge of karate gives you a physical advantage over others, you have a greater responsibility to avoid fights. This means practicing self-control so that you can ignore verbal threats, insults, and other challenges.

2. What should I do if I am threatened by someone or asked to fight?

The best response to a verbal threat is to ignore it. If your physical safety is threatened, however, you should act. Always respond to an aggressor with confidence. Look the person right in the eye to let him or her know that you are not afraid. Remain calm and look for a potential weak spot, such as a vulnerable standing position. If a fight does occur, you can take advantage of the weakness and end the fight with one move.

3. How do I build up my confidence so that I can stand up to an aggressor?

Confidence will come from knowing that the self-defense techniques you learn will work for you if you practice them. As you practice and show improvement, you will have more faith in your ability to defend yourself. It is this assurance that will enable you to stand up to an aggressor. Karate teaches that if you *believe* you can do something, you actually can do it.

4. What are the most important principles for karate students to remember and practice?

—Self-control must be maintained at all times.

—A fighting technique must never be used against another person unless you are in danger of being harmed.

—Along with increased strength and skill in fighting goes a greater responsibility to show kindness and respect toward other people.

5. Can I learn self-defense techniques by watching television and movies?

It is not a good idea to copy self-defense techniques shown on television or in the movies. Though they may be exciting, they do not work in real-life situations. Television programs and movies seek only to entertain and not to teach self-defense.

6. Should I let people know that I have studied self-defense so that they will respect me and think twice about picking a fight?

As a student of a fighting art, you should never brag or even talk about the self-defense skills you have learned. Such talk will only make enemies for you and may encourage someone to challenge you to a fight. Every serious student of self-defense concentrates instead on getting along with other people. If a fight should occur, that student will quietly use his or her self-defense skills to end the confrontation as soon as possible.

7. How long will it take me to become an expert in self-defense?

It takes many years of practice and hard work to become an expert in any field. This is especially true in the art of self-defense. Just reading books on the fighting arts is not enough to give a person the skill to become an expert. Students who are sincerely interested in becoming skilled at self-defense are encouraged to take classroom instruction from a qualified teacher. There are no shortcuts to learning self-defense. It requires time, effort, and constant practice.

1.

LIMBERING AND STRETCHING EXERCISES FOR KARATE

In order to perform the self-defense techniques of karate, it is necessary to condition the body with exercise. Exercise will make the body loose and flexible so that when the various techniques are practiced, the muscles will not be strained. The following exercises will provide the necessary conditioning for the muscle groups. It is recommended that you do these exercises before each practice session so that your body will be prepared for karate training.

Front Bending Exercise

From an erect posture, bend down and touch the palms of your hands against the ground. Try to do this without bending your knees.

Body Twisting Exercise

Spread your legs apart with your knees slightly bent. Extend your arms straight out to either side and twist at the waist as far as you can in each direction.

Leg Stretching Exercise

From a relaxed position with your feet together, kick one leg and then the other straight up without bending your knees. It is important to kick as high as possible.

Leaping Exercise

Squat on the floor and clasp your hands behind your back. Pushing from your toes, leap into the air as high as you can. (This exercise will condition your body for the flying side kick, which is shown in Chapter 7.)

Basic Flexibility Exercise

From a relaxed position, slowly spread your legs as far apart as possible and gradually ease yourself to the floor. *NOTE:* Do not stretch your muscles too much at one time. It is far better to do a little stretching each day and improve slowly than to exercise too fast and injure muscles.

2.

BASIC BODY MECHANICS AND SENSITIVE AREAS

Karate teaches that the entire body is used for self-defense. In making an attack, for example, the hands or feet are used to hit an aggressor. But only certain areas of the hands and feet actually make contact with the aggressor. The art of karate also teaches that certain parts of the body are more sensitive than others for *receiving* a strike or kick. A blow directed at one of these sensitive areas can stop an attacker immediately.

This chapter explains which areas of the hands and feet are used for self-defense. It also describes how to position the hands and feet for certain attacks. Also included are diagrams of the body's sensitive areas. These areas are considered the main striking areas in karate.

HAND POSITIONS FOR STRIKING

The Closed Fist

The closed fist can be used to attack the head, chest, and stomach of an aggressor.

In order to make a proper closed fist, fold your fingers tightly into your palm and place your thumb across the forefinger.

The first and second knuckles of your fist should make contact with the target.

The Open Hand

Tighten the open fingers of your hand by bending the tips slightly downward. Fold your thumb against your palm. When the blow is executed, the edge of the hand should make contact with the target. The open hand is used for striking the ribs, neck, or head of an aggressor.

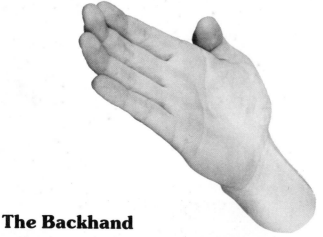

The Backhand

The position for the backhand is the same as for the closed fist. The striking areas, however, include the back of the hand and the knuckles. The backhand is used for attacking the chest and face of an aggressor.

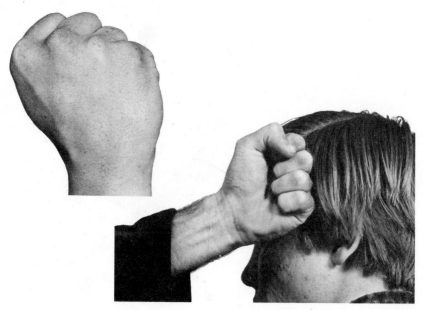

FOOT POSITIONS FOR KICKING

Kicks Using the Ball of the Foot

One part of the foot used for kicking an attacker is the ball, or the fleshy ridge at the base of the toes. When using the ball of your foot to stop an attacker, be sure to curl your toes upward so that they are not injured. Two kicks that use the ball of the foot are the front kick and the round kick. The ball of the foot is used for striking an attacker's groin, chest, or head.

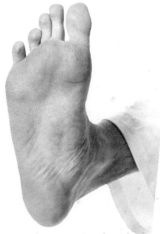

Kicks Using the Heel of the Foot

Another area of the foot used for kicking an attacker is the heel. When using this part of the foot, remember to curl your toes upward to avoid injury. Kicks using the heel of the foot include the side kick and the back kick. This foot area can be used for striking the groin, chest, or head of an attacker.

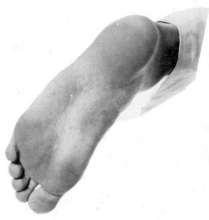

Chart of Sensitive Areas

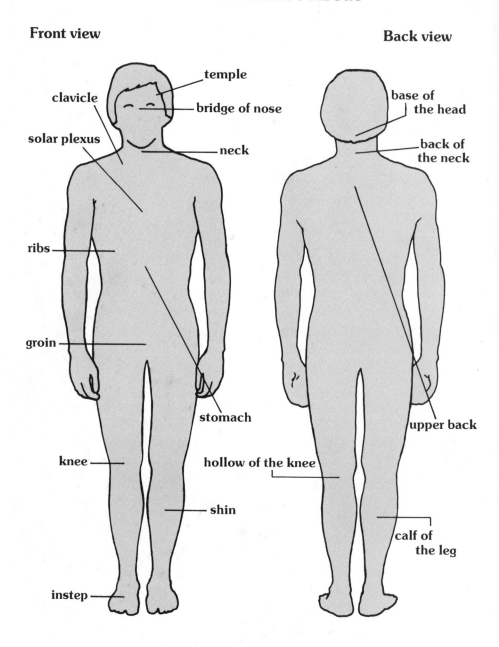

Front view

Back view

temple

clavicle

bridge of nose

solar plexus

neck

ribs

groin

stomach

knee

hollow of the knee

shin

instep

base of
the head

back of
the neck

upper back

calf of
the leg

3.

KARATE FIGHTING STANCES

The fighting stances are basic to the art of karate. These stances are the special standing positions from which the various fighting techniques—punching, blocking, and kicking—are performed. The positions serve to tense the muscles and also to strengthen them. In ancient times, karate students were forced to stay in their stances for many hours at a time in order to strengthen their legs. Though students of today are not required to do this, they still benefit from the strengthening effect of the stances as they practice.

It is important that your fighting stances are strong. If they aren't, you could easily be thrown off balance by your attacker. Weak stances can also make your defensive moves ineffective. In order to have a strong stance, you must practice two important principles of karate.

The first principle is known as *inner strength*. Inner strength is the ability to be aware of your own power and energy and to have control over it. To achieve inner strength you must concentrate, or focus your thoughts, on your lower stomach, where your power is centered. This concentration will result in a stance that is difficult for an aggressor to break. When you proceed to make a defensive move, such as a block or a strike, bring air up from your lower stomach and sharply exhale it through your nose and mouth. This action will distribute your power throughout your body.

The second principle involves using the power of your hip. When you are in a stance and you are about to throw a punch or a block, turn your hip in the direction of your attack. By doing this, you will throw your body weight into the attack and will therefore make the move very powerful.

This chapter describes the basic fighting stances of karate. Each stance should be learned thoroughly so that you can move from one stance to another with smooth, graceful motions.

The Horse Stance

The horse stance is the most basic stance in karate. It can be used for either attack or defense. The horse stance allows you a great deal of flexibility because you can easily move from it to any of the other fighting stances.

Learning Steps

1. Spread your feet apart and bend your knees much as you would if you were riding a horse.

2. Point your toes inward toward the opening between your legs.

3. Both hands should be made into fists and held at the waist, palms up.*

4. The upper half of your body should be erect, and your weight should be evenly distributed between both legs.

*NOTE: There are many different ways to hold the hands in the various fighting stances. Generally, it is best to keep both hands at waist level with at least one of them in a fist.

The Modified Horse Stance

The modified horse stance is used for either attack or defense. Almost any of the blocks, kicks, or punches in karate can be performed from this stance.

Learning Steps

1. Spread your legs apart, as in the horse stance, but do not face your attacker straight on.

2. Point your back foot slightly forward and your front foot slightly inward.

3. Make fists of both hands and hold them at waist level, palms up.*

4. Your body weight should be evenly distributed between both legs, and your knees should be bent slightly.

*NOTE: The hands can also be held as in the forward guarding stance, shown on the next page. One hand is in a fist held at the waist, while the other hand is open and extended forward, palm down.

The Forward Guarding Stance

This stance can be used for defense, but it is best suited for attack.

Learning Steps

1. Spread your legs wide apart, with one leg in front of the other.

2. The front leg should be bent slightly and should carry 60 percent of your body weight. The rear leg should be straight and should carry 40 percent of your body weight. Make sure that both heels are flat on the ground.

3. Turn the top half of your body toward your attacker.

4. Your right fist should rest on your hip, while your left fist should be held slightly out in front of your body in a guarding position.

The Basic Back Stance

The back stance is used primarily for defense. Students of karate should be able to shift quickly into the back stance if they are attacked.

Learning Steps

1. Place one leg in front of the other so that your feet are spread apart about twice the width of your shoulders.

2. The rear leg should be bent deeply and should carry about 70 percent of your weight. The front leg should be bent slightly and should carry only 30 percent of your weight.

3. The right fist should be resting at your hip, while the left hand should be kept open and held slightly in front of your body.

The Cat Stance

The cat stance is used for throwing very powerful front kicks.

Learning Steps

1. Stand with one leg directly in front of the other.

2. The rear leg should be planted firmly on the ground with the knee slightly bent and facing to the side. It should carry most of your body weight.

3. The front leg should be bent at the knee and balanced lightly on the ball of the foot. In this position it is free for throwing very fast kicks.

4. Both hands should be made into fists and carried at your sides.

4.

PROPER MOVEMENT FOR KARATE

The art of karate teaches that a person should always be physically well balanced, even when moving. There are three basic ways of moving in karate: sliding, body-shifting, and cross-stepping. By using these methods, you will be able to cover both large and small distances quickly, with a minimum of steps. You will also be physically well balanced.

Sliding

Sliding is usually best suited for covering short distances quickly. You can move forward, backward, or diagonally by sliding. Sliding can be done from the modified horse stance, the forward guarding stance, and the back stance.

Learning Steps

1. Starting in your stance, slide the front foot forward, and slide the back foot along behind.

2. Make sure that you maintain your fighting stance and that you are properly balanced.

Body-Shifting

Body-shifting movements are stepping movements that enable you to shift power from one side of your body to the other. These stepping movements also enable you to cover a large area quickly. Body-shifting can be done from any stance.

Learning Steps

1. Start from one of the fighting stances. Figure 1 shows the forward guarding stance.

2. Bring the rear leg forward until it is almost even with the other leg. By doing this, you are thrusting your hip forward and carrying your body weight into the move.

3. In a continuing motion, move the stepping leg forward and shift your body weight to it.

4. Throughout the movement, make sure that the supporting foot is planted firmly on the ground. Keep your posture erect and maintain good balance.

NOTE: This body-shifting movement shows the forward-stepping fore-fist punch, a hand technique explained in Chapter 6.

Cross-Stepping

Cross-stepping is used for moving to the right or the left and for covering great distances quickly. It is a movement that actually allows you to take a double step. Cross-stepping often confuses an aggressor, making it difficult for him or her to understand what you are going to do next. Cross-stepping is done most successfully from either the horse stance or the modified horse stance.

Learning Steps

1. Start from either the horse stance or the modified horse stance. Figure 1 shows the horse stance.

2. Move the stepping foot to the opposite side of the supporting foot and balance it on its toes. As you move, turn your head in the direction you are going.

3. In a continuing motion, shift your weight to the toes of your stepping foot and move your other foot farther to the side.

4. Finish as you began, in the horse stance.

WALLIS ELEMENTARY SCHOOL

5.

DODGING OR BLOCKING AN ATTACK

An important part of self-defense is knowing how to avoid an attacker's punch or kick. Karate teaches two ways of doing this: dodging and blocking. Either technique will protect you from an aggressor's blow until you can counterattack.

This chapter describes some of karate's basic dodging and blocking techniques. It is best to practice them with a partner. But if you do not have a partner, *imagine* that punches and kicks are being thrown at you by an attacker. Then practice dodging or blocking the attacks.

When practicing the blocks, go through them slowly at first and then quicken the pace. Only when you are confident that you can perform the blocking techniques well at both low and medium speeds should you attempt to practice them at fast speeds.

Dodging to the Side

Dodging to the side of a punch is an excellent self-defense technique. It is a good method to use when you are not in a fighting stance but are standing normally with your feet together. Use this dodge only when a punch is thrown at your neck or your head.

Learning Steps

1. As the aggressor releases the punch, bend the upper part of your body to one side.

2. Be sure to shift your weight in the direction you are bending so that you can maintain proper balance.

Dodging to the Rear

This dodge is used to evade a direct punch to the head. It is best performed from the modified horse stance.

Learning Steps

1. As the aggressor throws the punch toward your head, bend the upper part of your body backward. Keep your feet in position, but as you lean back shift your body weight to your rear leg.

2. The upper half of your body should move back fast enough so that the attacker's punch falls short of hitting you.

The Stepping-to-the-Rear Dodge

This dodge can be done from a normal standing position.

Learning Steps

1. As the attacker throws the punch, take a step backward so that you end in a modified horse stance.

2. As you move, bend the upper half of your body backward to avoid the punch.

LOWER-LEVEL-OF-THE-BODY BLOCKS

The Downward Block

The downward block is very useful for blocking attacks to the lower stomach and groin.

Learning Steps

1. Move the fist of the blocking arm to the opposite ear. Swing the arm downward so that the lower arm meets the attacker's punch or kick.

2. Your arm should be fully extended when it stops the attacker's punch or kick.

NOTE: Determine where you want your block to meet the aggressor's attack and focus on that point. By focusing, your block will be accurate and will have a great deal of power.

The Low Cross Block

The low cross block is very good for stopping kicks to the lower regions of the body. This block can be done from any of the fighting stances.

Learning Steps

1. Start from one of the fighting stances. Figure 1 shows the modified horse stance.

2. Cross your fists over the lower part of your body to meet the attack.

3. Try to keep the upper part of your body erect.

MIDDLE-OF-THE-BODY BLOCK

The Forearm Block

The forearm block is an extremely powerful block. It is used to stop punching attacks to the chest and stomach. Though the forearm block can be made from any stance, it is most effective from either the forward guarding stance or the modified horse stance.

Learning Steps

1. Start from one of the fighting stances. Figure 1 shows the forward guarding stance.

2. Bring your arm up from its lowered position with a strong snapping motion so that the inside edge of your arm meets the attacker's punching arm.

3. Your blocking arm must be bent sharply in order to withstand the force of the attacker's blow.

UPPER-LEVEL-OF-THE-BODY BLOCKS

The Rising Block

The rising block is used most often to defend against attacks to the head. This block can be done from any of the fighting stances.

Learning Steps

1. Start from one of the fighting stances. Figure 1 shows the modified horse stance.

2. Swing your front arm up in front of your head so that the soft part of your forearm faces out.

3. As the arm is brought upward, the soft part will block the attacker's punch.

The Upward Cross Block

The upward cross block can also be used to deflect attacks to the head. This block can be done from any of the fighting stances.

Learning Steps

1. Start from one of the fighting stances. Figure 1 shows the modified horse stance.

2. Move both arms upward and cross them at the wrists in front of your head. Keep both hands open, palms out, so that you can grasp the attacker's arm and make a counterattack.

3. In order for this block to have sufficient power, it is important that your elbows do not stick out beyond the width of your shoulders.

6.
HAND TECHNIQUES

The hands are very important in self-defense, for a well-placed blow can stop an attack immediately. The basic hand techniques in karate are punches and strikes. There is a difference between the two, and that difference is in the type of motion used. A punch involves a *thrusting* motion. When you punch, power is thrown from your shoulder and enters your hand. A strike involves more of a *snapping* motion. The power behind a strike is the result of the twisting, or snapping, of your elbow before the blow is delivered.

There are six punches and strikes in this chapter. Each one has a "form," or an orderly pattern of steps. By developing proper form in your hand techniques, you will have the necessary power to stop an attacker. The following principles will help you to develop that form:

First, focus on the spot you are attempting to hit. By keeping your eyes on the target, your blow will be accurate.

Second, use the inner strength techniques described in Chapter 3. These will strengthen your attack.

Third, use your hip power. Remember that by moving your hip in the direction of the attack, you will throw your body weight into the motion and will make the blow more powerful.

The Forefist Punch

The forefist punch is a very powerful hand technique that can be performed from any fighting stance. The punch starts from the side of the body. In mid-motion, the position of the fist is reversed to give more power to the attack.

Learning Steps

1. The punching fist should be held palm up just above the hip. The other hand should be fully extended, with the fingers open in a grabbing manner.

2. Throw the punching hand forward, reversing the position of the fist so that the palm is down and the knuckles are facing forward.

3. In the same motion, bring the outstretched arm back to the waist-level fist position.

NOTE: When practicing the hand techniques with a partner, *do not actually hit the person's body.* Stop the blow at least two inches (five centimeters) from the body.

The Forward-Stepping Forefist Punch

This is an even more powerful forefist punch because it involves the shifting of your body weight forward into the punch. This technique is used for attacking the upper part of the body. It is most often performed from either the modified horse stance or the forward guarding stance.

Learning Steps

1. Start from either the forward guarding stance (Fig. 1) or the modified horse stance.

2. Bring your back leg forward, and as it passes the front leg, throw a forefist punch.

3. Your leg and your fist should move forward at the same time, from the same side of the body. Your hip should be turned toward the attacker.

4. The stepping foot should end up in front of your body.

The Round Punch

The round punch is especially useful for attacking the side of an aggressor's body. It is most effective when an aggressor is standing very close to you. The round punch can be performed from any of the fighting stances.

Learning Steps

1. Start from one of the fighting stances. Figure 1 shows the modified horse stance.

2. Hold your punching fist slightly above your hip and thrust it outward in a slight curve so that it hits the side of the attacker's body.

3. In the same motion, move the other hand to your waist in a palm-up fist position.

The Backfist Strike

The backfist strike is a powerful technique used for attacking the head or chest of an aggressor. The backfist is most often performed from the forward guarding stance or the modified horse stance.

Learning Steps

1. Start from either the forward guarding stance or the modified horse stance, with your attacking fist held at your waist.

2. With a quick snap of your elbow, bring your forearm upward so that the back of your fist strikes the target.

The Open-Hand Strike

The open-hand strike is especially useful for attacking the neck or ribs of an aggressor. This strike can be done most successfully from either the forward guarding stance or the modified horse stance.

Learning Steps

1. Start from either the forward guarding stance or the modified horse stance. Figure 1 shows the modified horse stance.

2. Shift hand positions by placing the striking hand next to the ear on the opposite side of your body.

3. The striking hand should be in the open hand position explained in Chapter 2.

4. The other hand should extend slightly forward, the palm facing the attacker.

5. Swing the striking hand forward in the direction of the target. In mid-motion, reverse the position of the hand so that the palm faces down. The outside edge of your hand will strike the target.

The Elbow Strike

The elbow strike can be used in many self-defense situations. It is generally used when an aggressor is very close to you and you want to throw him or her off guard. The following illustration shows the elbow strike as a technique for stopping an attack from behind. When practicing the elbow strike, it is a good idea to work with a partner and to practice the technique from as many attacking situations as you can think of.

Learning Steps

1. As the aggressor grabs you from behind, swing your elbow, hip, and leg backward with a great deal of force.

2. Your elbow should strike the aggressor in the face or the side of the head.

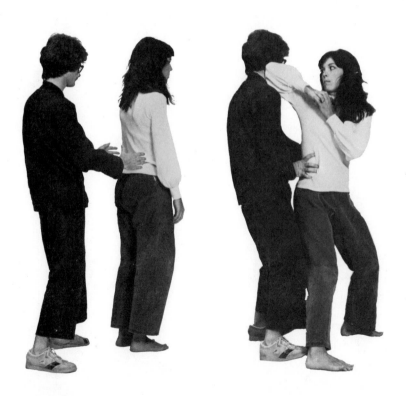

7.

KICKING TECHNIQUES

Kicking techniques are useful for self-defense because the human leg is very strong and can be a powerful weapon. Because the leg has a long reach, a kick can also be done from a safer distance than a punch or strike. An effective kick depends on three things. First, the supporting leg must be bent slightly and planted firmly on the ground. Second, proper balance must be maintained throughout the kick. And third, the power of the hip should always be used.

The following techniques are basic kicking techniques in karate. They can be done from any of the fighting stances. When practicing these techniques with a partner, do not actually kick the other person. Stop the kick at least two inches (five centimeters) from your partner's body.

The Front Kick

The front kick is a powerful foot technique that can be used for either defense or attack. It is used to strike an aggressor's knees, groin, stomach, or head.

Learning Steps

1. Bend the knee of the kicking leg and lift it toward your chest. Turn the toes upward so that they will not be injured when your foot hits the target.

2. Thrust the kicking leg forward and hit your target with the ball of your foot.

3. After the target has been hit, return your leg to the bent knee position. If there is no need to throw additional kicks, return to a normal standing position.

NOTE: These steps should be practiced until the kick can be done in one smooth, powerful motion.

The Side Kick

As the name suggests, the side kick is made from the side of the body. It is an especially powerful technique for defense. The side kick can be used against the knees, groin, stomach, or head of an aggressor.

Learning Steps

1. Lift the kicking leg and hold it next to the supporting leg, bent at the knee. Be sure that your toes are turned upward.

2. Thrust the kicking leg out to the side of your body, and hit the target with the heel of your foot.

3. After the target has been hit, return your leg to the bent knee position. If there is no need to throw additional kicks, return to a normal standing position.

The Back Kick

The back kick is used to defend against attacks from the rear. It is very important to maintain proper balance throughout the back kick.

Learning Steps

1. Lift the kicking leg toward your chest and turn your head so that you can see behind you.

2. Thrust the kicking leg straight back, and strike your target with the heel of your foot.

3. When the target has been hit, return your leg to the bent knee position. If there is no need to throw additional kicks, shift into a fighting stance.

The Round Kick

The round kick will surprise an attacker because it will hit where it is least expected—on the side of the body. This kick is especially suited for attacking an aggressor's head, neck, or ribs.

Learning Steps

1. Start from the modified horse stance, as shown in Figure 1.

2. Shift your weight to the front leg as you swing your back leg around toward the attacker. The leg should be bent at the knee and held away from your body, parallel to the ground.

3. In a continuing motion snap your kicking leg outward, hitting your target with the ball of your foot.

4. After striking the target, return your leg to the bent knee position. If there is no need to throw additional kicks, return to the modified horse stance.

The Stamping Kick

The stamping kick involves the bottom of the foot. It is a useful technique for striking the knee, shin, or foot of an aggressor. The stamping kick can also be used to distract an aggressor so that a middle-level or high-level body punch can be thrown without being blocked.

Learning Steps

1. Raise the kicking leg toward your chest.

2. Thrust it downward so that your heel strikes the target.

The Flying Side Kick

The flying side kick can be used for hitting an aggressor's upper body. It is a dramatic technique that is executed from the side of the body.

Learning Steps

1. Start from the horse stance. Be sure to look in the direction that you are going to kick.

2. Leap high into the air, drawing both legs close to your body.

3. Thrust the leg closest to the aggressor straight out to the side. Make sure that the other foot is drawn up close to the kicking leg.

4. Strike the target with the heel of your kicking foot. Land in a strong stance so that you can continue to defend yourself if necessary.

The Basic Ground Kick

This technique enables a person on the ground to fight off an aggressor who is standing. A properly executed ground kick often catches an aggressor by surprise because he or she does not expect the downed person to keep on fighting.

Learning Steps

1. From your position on the ground, draw your knees toward your chest. Your feet should be facing the attacker, and your hands should be flat against the ground, bracing your body.

2. Thrust one leg and then the other toward the aggressor's shins, knees, groin, or stomach.

3. Do not get off the ground until the aggressor has retreated. When you are standing again, prepare to use hand techniques if your foot technique has not stopped the attack.

SAFETY RULES

Proper safety precautions must always be taken when practicing karate techniques. The main thing to remember is that a practice session is not the same as an actual fight. It is simply a time when students can work together to improve their self-defense skills. The following list of safety rules has been developed to reduce the risk of personal injury during practice sessions.

1. Be sure to do the warm-up exercises before each practice session. If you don't, you could easily pull a muscle.

2. Do not try to stretch your muscles too much at any given time. It is far better to condition your muscles gradually than to do too much at once and injure them.

3. During your practice sessions, do not actually hit your partner. When practicing a punch, a strike, or a kick, stop the blow at least two inches (five centimeters) from your partner's body.

INDEX

ABOUT THE AUTHOR

Fred Neff has been a student of the Asian fighting arts for most of his life. He started his training at the age of eight and eventually specialized in karate. Today Mr. Neff holds the rank of fifth degree black belt in that fighting art. In addition to karate, he is also proficient in judo and jujitsu. For many years, Mr. Neff has used his knowledge of the Asian fighting arts to educate others. He has taught karate at the University of Minnesota, the University of Wisconsin, and Hamline University and Inver Hills College in St. Paul, Minnesota. He has also organized and supervised self-defense classes in public schools, private schools, and in city recreation departments. Included in his teaching program have been classes for law enforcement officers.

Fred Neff graduated with high distinction from the University of Minnesota College of Education in 1970. In 1976, he received his J.D. degree from William Mitchell College of Law in St. Paul, Minnesota. Mr. Neff is now a practicing attorney in Minneapolis, Minnesota.

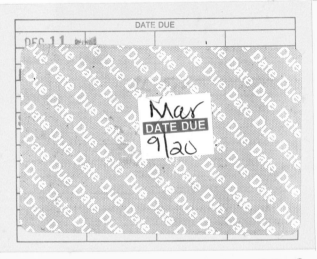